Beauty I Feel...

Melissa Brown

BookLeaf
Publishing

Presentation by *BookLeaf Publishing*

Web: www.bookleafpub.com

E-mail: info@bookleafpub.com

ISBN: 9789357445795

First edition 2023

To my Mom, the most beautiful and perfect mother and Godly example who inspires me to be just like her even when she's telling me that I can be more. These moments of beauty I can see because you taught me how to look. I love you!

ACKNOWLEDGEMENT

I have to say a huge Thank You to my fellow writer and poet Francis Maffi-Mahmood, one of my very best friends, who always encourages and inspires me to keep pushing and imagining and using my creative side. Without her enthusiasm, feedback, editing eyes, and kindred spirit, my belief in the value of my own voice would still be dim. We did it, my friend!

PREFACE

In the words of Percy B. Shelley: "Poetry lifts the veil from the hidden beauty of the world and makes familiar objects be as if they were not familiar."

I've always loved that the right words can take a moment of unique memory or thought and transform it into a communal experience of emotion that's elaborate, engaging, and emphatic. I am forever fascinated by the vastness and intricacies of the world and strive never to take for granted the beauty of life itself, in the light and in the dark. Every person has the ability to find these moments of hidden beauty in life, and I hope that sharing mine will make those "familiar objects" just a little more beautiful.

That being said, I also have long been enamored and challenged by all different styles of verse, the limitless modes of playing with rhythm, rhyme, imagery, and structure. You'll find in these pages not only an exploration of moments in my life but also of the inventive and adaptive styles that have inspired me and given my soul a voice. Every poet has a style, and mine has always been as eclectic as my experiences.

In the words of Edgar Allan Poe: "I would define, in brief, the poetry of words as the rhythmical creation of beauty."

In my words...

Reading poetry can truly be
like reading a diary,
purest expression on each line
of heart and mind to see.

As color and brush stroke reveals
an artist's mood and person,
so does the rhythm and the rhyme
and flow the poet's verses.

Yet such revealing of the self
with fear, nerves intertwined,
such revelation of the self
leaves one open to being maligned.

Every line and every beat,
all rhyme and imagery
act as the full and perfect moon,
reflecting the sunlight in me.

A single verse of poetry
a beautiful story does tell,
so climb aboard the poet’s mind:
don’t worry, the tides will swell
and sail you to a magic place
where dreams and life combine,
within the poet’s verse is fraught
fantasy of space and time.

Only hesitate when psalm is done,
‘tis on a journey the reader goes,
don’t stop for rest or noon repast,
don’t wish for wordy prose.

Know the poet in every phrase,
shimmering moonlight reaching down,
fall in love with the art of words,
views of life at once profound.

Reading poetry is such a gift
for reader and bard alike:
The poet’s soul can light a path
by which reader can find respite.

Here’s to this beauty I feel!

Beauty to Find...

God's glorious creation,
all things for life's joy,
Do I stop and take the time
my heart and mind employ?

Noticing the autumn leaf
drift resignedly to the ground,
breathing in rich, winter air
wrapped by breezes that surround,

a wagging tail, a gentle purr,
a dripping chorus of rain,
a russet purple sunset,
used dishwater down a drain,

kindred spirits to understand,
a friend to know me well,
a joy and beauty all my own
within my soul does swell.

Extraordinary, surpassing, infinite
is what God's beauty is,
no single soul can fathom
its depth in this world of His.

We each must seek and recognize
the beauty of our lives,
spreading wide like wildflowers
the joy given to us by
every little moment and big
whereby we realize
that finding His beauty in our unique ways
fulfills life's purpose, the ultimate prize.

Beauty's Foundation-In God: Do We Get That?

Christ came and was allowed to suffer, die and be glorified "…that your faith and hope might be in God." (I Pet. 1:18-21)

In God.
Do we get that?

A few seconds of thought,
two syllables,
infinite meaning,
All meaning,
All Truth
In God.
Bible says
All things
are His,
For Him,
Because of Him,
To Him,
In Him.
In God.
Life itself,
breath itself,

galaxies themselves,
Exist
In God.
Faith and hope,
things unseen,
things abstract,
evidence of meaning,
existential meaning.
Do we get that?
That God
wants creation
to know Him,
Inconceivable.
That God
wants creation
to hope in Him,
Unfathomable.
That God
wants creation
to put faith in Him,
Inexplicable.
Do we get that?
In God,
reality is,
we're all
In God
as creations. Our being
held in His hand.
But our faith

and hope
in God
changes it all.
In God,
our being is already.
Do we get that?
In God,
our faith saves.
Jesus was raised
"That (our) faith and
hope might be…"
Jesus is proof.
His sacrifice
displays eternally
a depth, a nature of love,
God's perfect love.
Do we get that?
In God,
our hope should be
Because…
Because…
By reason of…
His cross,
His life,
His death,
His resurrection.
God desires to be known.
Do we get that?
To know Him

is to see faith and hope
fulfilled entirely.
To see Him,
To know Him,
To acknowledge Truth,
To recognize
ALL is IN GOD!
"For His pleasure we are and were
created."
Do we get that?
"In Him,
we live
and move
and have
our being…"
The God,
we are His already.
He is God…already.
Do we get that?
His supremacy
unchallenged.
His power
indisputable.
In God,
not just location,
a habitation,
a home for our hopes,
our dreams,
our faith,

our trust,
our surrender.
Jesus died for
our surrender,
our submission
to Himself.

Jesus died
that we might find
ourselves forever
In God.
Do we get that?

Haiku Childhood

middle child of three
independent, wished to be
never rebellious

countless metal chairs
mother playing piano
dad at the pulpit

singing with sister
what they all seem to require
hypocrites and saints

little brother pest
why won't he leave me alone
go play with April

learning all at home
many friends around for me
centered by the church

hours of play outside
big backyard, imagined worlds
library next up

books for me to read
stories loved all on my own
my fantasy world

family vacations
road trip, northbound, Iowa
pizza on white tow'ls

moved away at 12
no more friends for me to love
God Himself shown real

never seen for me
was not thin or pretty one
then he saw me there

felt alone so long
life's unfair to bear at times
peace still soothes my soul

life's details prepared
strength to lean, trust all His plans
beauty now unleashed

Faithful Creator

Faithful Creator,
a fitting title to bear.
Beginnings from Your Word
out of literally nowhere.

By You and for You
All things came to be,
Your pleasure be our purpose
since before the fateful tree.

Our submission deserved
Terrible power us could subdue,
But Your nature frees,
Amazing grace is Your purview.

Created to be useful,
glorifying to Your name,
without that truth accepted
we've nothing left but shame.

Our terrestrial existence
our choice didn't require:
Our view then of this life
as ours, we must retire.

So who's this One we worship?
The Creator God above:
the One who chose all things,
Himself, the source of Love.

A Teacher's Fairytale

Once upon a time,
a girl began to teach.
She loved her books and stories,
students she wanted to reach.

First year finally down,
exhausted to her core,
some friends could not endure to live
in this kingdom she adored.

She worked and worked to lead them,
scant appreciation in sight.
She loved and built and guided,
for students she was a light.

Long days and months, years endured,
stresses growing every day,
pressures mounting from enemy kings,
creating pitfalls along the way.

She went to shores Down Under,
new stories she thought to tell,
but disrespect a fierce dragon found,
fire breathing ne'er do wells.

Returning from far, far away
the teacher sought true love again.
But plague across the land did rage,
home from the classroom sent.

Locked away with a magic mirror
and wishing to be free,
this teacher felt under a spell,
could fairest love from early on be key?

Finally, her joyful kingdom
found its plague destroyed,
yet harsh effects were far and wide,
testing every girl and boy.

Hopeful eyes meeting hers,
a nervous smile, some fears,
she saw her reason to survive,
striving through her students' tears.

But scorching, changing monarchies
couldn't dim the glowing fire
of students' minds finding answers
and the stories they inspire.

No magic wand, no fairies,
no witch who cast a spell,
this teacher rediscovered fair love:
Despite war, her kingdom's well.

A Beautiful Shift...

Sometimes it feels
Like life is just spinning right on by me,
Crazily flying by like
So many pinwheels in a hard, west wind.
Times come and things change and I
Wonder what life still holds in store.
Moments arise
When the kisses of sun on my skin
Alone keep me warm;
Then there are moments when the cool breath
Of the unknown seems to seep into my mind,
Dripping icicles falling from tree branches.
Life is moving, yet
Where is it going?
Does one ever know?
Does one ever
Really get to know what lies ahead?
Not until the end, will all things be revealed,
At least that's what I've been taught.
Quietness and a need for rest
Overtake my anxious and
Fantastical imaginations.

But, then a light,
A spark of color in a sea of dull grey,

A piece of peace breaking through the mist that
has settled on my heart and mind.
My eyes open as I take in the widening dawn,
The hazy, rosy, red/orange sun
Struggling through the horizon for freedom,
It is an awakening, a new understanding.
It is a knowledge that dulls
The unknown into oblivion,
An element that allows life
To move seamlessly into
A comforting, joyful reality.

Where is life going?
Do I know?
Not yet, but that sensation doesn't hold
The crimson anxieties it used to hold.
Soothing petals of pink and leaves of green
Touch the edges of my existence
Denoting the reviving of life within me.
What is this change and
How did it happen?
What light broke through, lifting
The fog of fear and its effects?
There was that light,
That burst of brilliance,
Changing the dark night
To glowing morning.
What was that change?
What brought meaning and certainty,

Delight and ecstasy, happiness and purpose
To a life void of a rudder,
Void of roses and passion pink.
What was the change
That made all the difference,
Changing one sleeping into one vividly alive?
That change….
Was YOU!

His Inviting

We blink,
the day is gone.
Moon is rising,
but the work's not done.

Frantic, busy,
no time to stop,
the world so briskly spinning,
when will the hammer drop?

So many lives,
they're out of control.
Are they seeking Him
or just more idols?

We see the pain.
Heartache fills the room.
We know the cure,
And it's not in a tomb.

Time escapes
its prison with the dawn;
a new day begins
untouched yet by demons.

Just wait a moment,
one hour, maybe two,
Those demons seem
to rise as if on cue.

We thought that we could breathe
a sigh of life in peace,
but the left makes very sure
there's rioting instead of sleep.

Rest is found in Him
who sits upon His throne,
found in Him who's worthy
of all our praise alone.

So to His throne we run
trying just to survive,
yet find in the Light of Him
we feel our souls revive.

Life so very callous,
unfeeling and dangerous,
but it cannot overcome
the price He paid for us.

We are sealed and purchased,
stamped by royal blood.
We can be victorious
even drowning in a flood.

He called worlds into existence:
His power controls all things.
Oh sweet the rest we find in Him:
The peace at His inviting!

Hidden in the Rainforest

Vantage point more than ten stories high,
rainforest as far as eye can see,
deepest and rarest greens blend in harmony
innumerable trees,
infinite numbers of dew drops create crystal
sparkles on the vastness of leaves,
it feels as though the earth has taken you into
itself,
humming with life,
expelling growth as simply and easily as a
breath-
the soft blue of the sky takes second place here,
a bird's call echoes and finds its answer,
soldiers lined up, moving in sync- armies
    of ants crawl over each limb caught swaying
Vantage on the ground again, a canopy
overhead-
towering tree trunks so thick, so tall, only small
swathes of sun
    dare push through,
limbs and leaves intertwining yards above the
ground,
plants climbing each other,
vines weaving against trees,
    against bushes,

searching for the light,
creeping upward, pushing, clawing
    against each other to reach it.
Breathe in, and rich oxygen invades the nostrils-
so much life, so much
    hidden…
tree tops lush with health
    while shrubbery suffers in shadows-
Is that the cry of a wild boar?
Be wary of the slithering serpent slipping
silently through the brush-
Danger here clings with the vines,
Yet mysterious riches hidden, no man to find-
Breathe in the beauty of
    sacred space,
vast is the glory here,
unsearchable,
barely knowable,
it is Majesty.

Where's our Answer?

Echoing voices,
drowning in a mire of pain,
Why us? How could you?
Where's our answer? their hearts demand.
Take a breath, His Word responds.

Questions have answers,
All balances reconciled.
All creation sings
In One who came meek and mild
In One sitting on His throne.

Deny majesty,
denying His sovereignty,
All authority
belongs solely unto Him,
Lord and Christ of all the earth.

They run but can't hide.
The thunder of His voice shakes
them from their hiding,
No, never to be denied,
Jealous God of all the earth.

Where are our answers?

They cry, insolent children,
yet ignore His Word
and Truth revealed long ago,
clearly explained yet unseen.

Promises steadfast,
the God of all tomorrows,
upheld in His palm.
Response we seek may be soft,
quiet in the storms of life.

Who must answer us?
Who are we to demand that?
Did we purpose life?
Why should God answer to us?
Did we speak life from nothing?

How dare we demand
that God makes us feel at ease
with choices He's made!
How dare we think He's not good
when we don't see His full plan.

People want answers,
yet surrender is the key
that unlocks the door,
opening a world of peace
relying solely on Him.

In that place of peace,
His perfect goodness answers
those questions we have.
His very nature tells us
the answers to those questions.

He Himself is Good.
He can never be weakened,
His Will will be done,
for all of life rests in Him,
Lord and Christ of all the earth.

He Himself is Good.
All He does by nature Good.
Problem is not Truth.
The problem is in our trust.
Trusting Him, not in ourselves.

If we want answers,
we must take God at His Word:
By faith made perfect,
God's perfected creations,
knowing Him the full answer.

Jael

Being home,
Wrapped in snow,
Laughter flows,
Moonlight shows.

Content to be
luxuriously
stuck inside,
away from pride.

My daughter's face
illuminating space,
stars in her eyes,
innocence resides.

My favorite girl
in the whole wide world,
makes life sublime;
in shadow, you still shine.

Fresh Start

Wind whistles through tree branches,
A chill breathing along the breeze,
Dew drops resting on dark petals,
Drenched branches stretched from trees:

The world feels fresh and clean; it's ready for something new.
Though tension's high and heavy, Creation demands its own ado.

God can be a fire, consuming all He sees,
yet He refreshes His people, like ripples in the seas.

Within Him, we live
and move and are.
As the promise of Spring,
our Hope is never far.

This Thing, So New

There is something without a name
Floating in the air.
It is light like hummingbird wings,
Sweet like melted chocolate,
The color of rainbows in a spring rain.
It is the sensation of home:
Comfort, Joy, Peace.

It is the breathed sigh escaping a long kiss.
It is the sparkles dancing in the air,
Heightened emotions,
Roses in constant bloom.

As pieces of you meld into
Pieces of me,
I think only of you and a name
Comes to me,
A name so tempered,
Gold with steel overlaid.

This thing, so new, its reality
Eludes still in many moments,
But as time passes and
I taste this thing in your kisses,
It is constantly reiterated;

Forever I’m reminded
Of this thing that fills
Each flower with color,
Each meal with flavor,
Each cloud with silver,
Each rain with power,
Each heartbeat with rhythm,
Each second with purpose and magic,
Each breath with the splendor of days ever new

This THING
Called being in love with YOU…

With you...

A voice in solidarity,
A moment of understanding,
An instant of connection
that goes beyond pandering.

You're a barn light on a fog filled night.
You're a sense of relief when tensions are tight.

A smile that goes
deep behind our eyes,
a purpose far beyond
the means that we espy.

A heart that longs to see every life succeed,
sometimes just a little faith is all we really need.

Knowing that we're really
doing this thing together
makes the trials feel lighter,
as if they're only feathers.

Vision Incomplete

heart's desire
a family grown,
loneliness crashes
on shores not seeming home

hearts cry in need
vision incomplete,
anchored in Goodness
yet feeling adrift in grief

Love truly met
with loss intertwined,
for He is perfect Love,
control cannot be mine…

though waves they crash
and emotions storm,
still Love is there,
extraordinary, perfect in form

heart's lonely cries
become heart's praises
as agony surrenders,
a ship's white flag it raises

losing my place
as my life's sovereign
in this I found
my heart's sight finally opened
to all the abundance
solely found in Him,
like deeply buried treasure,
such riches I did WIN

heart's desires
a family fulfilling
our purpose blood bought
owed the only righteous King

hearts cry with joy
vision still incomplete,
but…stronger faith found every day
by His majesty replete

Daddy/Daughter Game

Daddies and their daughters,
few relationships as complex,
needing to be seen and heard,
neither what the other expects.

A lovely dance of circumstance
some lucky, some in despair,
easy for a dad to think
it doesn't matter if he cares.

But oh the riven wound that's left
on a daughter's sight and worth
when daddies leave off love and time
and sharing simple mirth.

Video games and inside jokes,
the teasing all day long,
these sweetest bonds of value forged
give stability and make her strong.

Though daddies often make dumb jokes
and prefer to play around,
those games he plays insurance be
that her ship won't run aground.

Daughters need their daddies,
he's the first love she will know,
she needs attention with real respect,
toward what's modeled she will go.

But daddies need daughters just as much
though they may deny the truth,
a daughter's pure devotion
his edges uniquely smooth.

A mother's love is powerful.
Its import can't be denied,
but a daddy's love prods and shoves
and gives wings for flying high.

like the moon, my heart...

dark of night, a cloudless sky
a brilliant, full moon's perfection
questions arise between our hearts
questions of introspection

am I ever a disappointment?
tremulous emotion seeks real reply,
can the stars above be disappointed
when the moon at times is shy?

tonight it shines its glory down,
its reflection of sunlight complete,
potential fulfilled this starry night,
inspiring the weary's dreams

as beautiful as moonlight is
through phases it waxes and wanes,
some days the dark of moonless night
forgets the light will come again

the moon never worries itself
when it doesn't reflect that light,
it simply holds itself in place
awaiting time to be just right

as ones with moonlight so enthralled
we don't the darkness fear,
for faith recalls that moonlight shines
when heaven's pathways clear

am I ever a disappointment?
you've asked for truth from me,
how could disappointment rise?
even hidden, your light I see

tomorrow's moon may not appear
as bright as seen before,
but confidence is never dimmed
that its radiance will be restored

just like the moon, my heart, I feel
your question's a dazzling blessing,
for in those thoughts with sunlight glow,
I feel your honest wishing

just like the moon, my heart, you are
revolving through life's phases,
and like the moon, my heart, I know
your value never changes

like the moon, my heart, please know
disappointment can only come
if your presence ceased to be,
only by absence sorrow begun

dark of night, this cloudless sky,
the moon a vivid sight,
your shine, my heart, can’t be denied:
don’t doubt your purpose bright.

Playful Dream

my daughter's dream
a pet to love,
bad luck to overcome.

a predator
at times a friend,
a feline not a chum.

off to shelter
one day we went,
we wondered what we'd find.

an orphaned cat,
a kitten pal,
this dream won't leave her mind.

bounding antics,
precious laughter,
attention day and night.

such bliss alit
with beauty sit,
her dreams with purrs take flight.

...checkpoint...

a long journey,
part way there,
God is faithful,
casting all care…

day by day
choices are hard,
moving forward,
feeling from heart…

the mind in battle,
many fronts,
focused offensives,
eschewing dunce…

visible progress,
thankful to be
taking the hill
toward victory…

checking in,
half to the goal,
mind on Him,
His grace bestowed…

Faces of Friendship

connected in childhood,
pastoring parents, purr-fect passions, and peanut
M&Ms
so many memories,
sleepovers and shared dreams,
phases and failings, years and yearnings,
pouring out in pages upon pages of letters,
experiences mount and
wisdom grows,
forged finely by minutes, miles, missing you,
and making moments
distance doesn't dim…

connected in college,
time to find ourselves
sharing learning, in pages and off
working on waiting for perfection
working on who we're going to be,
believe in potential,
believe in power,
feel confidence in kindred spirits
do you see him smile?
pay attention to forever.
peers and professionals, now veterans,
still striving, still vying for perfection

daily demands don't dim…

connected by caring,
teenagers spreading our wings,
high school a memory,
but years beyond brought a bond,
two birds flying high, far from the nest
always provided each other a place to land,
never demanding yet always finding fun and
fellowship
solidarity in support of moments that mattered,
reminiscent of home, yet
experiencing the world
ready always with prayer and excitement
separate lives keeping apart, yet
delayed dates don't dim…

connected by calling,
partners in ministry
far from family and familiar
yet hearts find home,
healing holidays and hopeful work,
sharing the hard
lonely laundry drying on the line,
sharing the happy
sparkling, soothing seashores,
forever family now for the foreign experience
ministry changes and home moves on,
calling shifts,

bonds do not,
divergent paths don't dim…

these faces of friendship
bring beauty to all my moments,
for Love has a knack for noticing what's needed
most
and friendship fills in the facets of fracture
that without would only be left maimed and
marred
despair doesn't dim…
damage doesn't dim…
drama doesn't dim…
disappointment doesn't dim…
even death could never dim…
these faces of Friendship!

I'm Not Always...

I'm not always the strong one, though I've
learned how to be.
I'm not always the gracious one, though I hold
back on many things.
I'm not always the one with answers, but His
Word gives me clarity.
I'm not usually perfect, though I try so hard to
be.
I'm not the one with unmet needs; God's grace is
sufficient for me.
Though many times I've wished for one to
understand,
That wish is only fulfilled from the palm of His
outstretched hand.
So I'm not always the strong one because God
has to be.
So I'm not always the gracious one, His Spirit
though moves in me.
I don't have all the answers, but I know the One
who does.
I can't possibly be perfect, thank God for His
forgiving love.
I don't have any unmet needs because God
knows what's best.

Being known by my Creator God simply covers all the rest.

When Beauty's Found (Philippians 4:4)

When beauty is found, no matter the moment,
one final task is mine...answer it back with joy!

Rejoice.
Re. Joy.
Respond to joy.
Reply to joy.
Feel and experience joy.
Rejoice is response,
Response to that which is given already.

Joy is a fruit, not a tree.
I am not a tree.
I can't produce joy.
So what flowers in joy?
It's a fruit, a fruit of the Spirit, the Holy Spirit alone.

Rejoice.
Re. Joy.
Reply to joy as it blooms,
as it grows and builds.
The Comforter has come,
Rejoice!

Joy surrounds, follows, and streams from
He who wants and sees all who wait.
His Spirit brings joy with His purpose.
His Spirit brings joy with our futures.
Joy envelops us with His presence and promises.
Rejoice.
Respond to joy that is set before us.

To rejoice is…
to answer back
all that's already set before.
"Rejoice in the Lord always,
and again, I say, Rejoice."
Rejoice.
Reply to Joy IN Joy WITH Joy
of Him.

He is Good. All He is
by nature
Good. Joyful
despite darkness,
despite pain,
despite fear,
despite heartbreak,
for all…all things
have a purpose,
A beautiful purpose!

Life teaches
this Goodness
if we let it,
if we rejoice in
what He's given,
what He's shown
of Himself
and His glory
and His Goodness.
Respond to life with Joy.
Rejoice.
Re. Joy.
Rejoice Always!

www.ingramcontent.com/pod-product-compliance
Lightning Source LLC
Chambersburg PA
CBHW051737130826
49812CB00033B/895
9789357445795